HOW I MAKE SIX FIGURES PLAYING WITH DOG HAIR

10 STEP GUIDE TO START YOUR PET GROOMING BUSINESS

JANELLE RUSSELL

How I Make Six Figures Playing with Dog Hair

10 Step Guide to Start Your Pet Grooming Business

Copyright © 2021 by Janelle Russell

Print ISBN: 978-1-952561-16-0

Get It Done Publishing, LLC.

Atlanta, GA 30349

www.getitdonepublishing.com

Printed in the United States of America.

INTRODUCTION

This book will provide the ten steps I took to start my pet grooming business—the ups and downs, highs, and lows. I'll explain all of the trials and tribulations I experienced with entrepreneurship. My goal is that my story will propel you in your journey with your business so you can avoid the mistakes I made within mine.

As far as I can remember, I've always had a love for dogs. In 1997, my best friend Barbara Ann and I saw a tail-less cat on Bouldercrest Road. We pulled over and captured it, then went back and forth, trying to figure out who would take care of it. At the time, Barbara already had a cat, so it was me who had to hide it in my basement. It took about three weeks until my mom figured out why I was trotting downstairs with food, water, and blankets every hour. Once she saw my surprise, she giggled and said, "I knew you had an animal down here!"

We took the cat to the local shelter, where she was placed in a forever home. It was years later until I had a real dog of my own. My boyfriend at the time gifted me an Apricot Toy Poodle for my twenty-fifth birthday. It was love at first sight—he was the cutest little thing. From that moment on, he was my baby, and I had to protect and spoil him at all cost. At the time, I worked for Corporate America in the banking industry and loved my job. I was making enough money to take care of myself and my lifestyle, but something changed when this little four-legged fur baby came into my life. I felt like I needed more out of life. I stayed with my job for another four years, and on my anniversary, I was fired. Was I sad or upset? No. I had a gut feeling it was going to happen sooner or later. I remember sitting in my car in the parking lot thinking to myself, *"Okay, Janelle. Now what?"*

The days ahead weren't the best, but I made it through. I had to apply for unemployment. Getting three hundred and twenty-five dollars per week helped a lot, considering I had a mortgage, car note, and utilities. But in this new chapter, I had more than enough free time. That was great because my best friend, Janae, had quit her job too. What a coincidence! We went to lunch one day, and while we were eating, we asked one another what we would do next. Then we looked at each other and said, "We should become entrepreneurs." Janae already had an idea of what she wanted to do, but I didn't. I went home thinking, what is it that I love doing and could make money? What is my passion? What's my craft? I was thinking all of this while rubbing my fur baby JJ. Then a lightbulb went off in my head! *Ding dong—dog groomer. I want to open a dog spa.*

Over the years, I've spent so much money on JJ's grooming. Every time I would pick him up from the groomers, he would hide under the bed for at least two days. It was a service I knew he needed, but I always had a lingering sense of frustration after it was done. As much as I loved making sure JJ was groomed, I didn't like the trade-off of the emotional toll it took on him. So, he became my reason and my motivation. He was always there when I needed to talk and always there to comfort me when I cried, was sad, or an emotional wreck. JJ was there through many boyfriends and breakups, from marriage to divorce, and babyless and carefree, to baby and on lockdown! When I thought about how much JJ mattered to me and how much I knew the grooming experience mattered to other pet owners, it made perfect sense to build off that. How I started and ran my business would be how I wanted JJ to feel when he got groomed. I wanted a place not stressful and scary but fun, safe, clean, and enjoyable. That's when all the brainstorming and planning began.

CONTENTS

1

VISION

Every person in life has a vision. Some will execute theirs, and some will fail. But for me, my vision for my life changed many times. By the time I figured I wanted to open a pet grooming salon, I had wasted a couple of years. I felt old entering the pet industry, so I had to put my thoughts into motion. Once I had the idea, I had to visualize how I wanted my business to look and run. What could I do to make my shop different? Location, mobile versus brick and mortar, business name, logo, colors, website, funding, equipment, etc., the planning part could be very overwhelming. However, for me, it was exciting! It took about six months to really sit down and think about what I wanted and how I would get it done. Also, in this phase, I prayed a lot. I wanted to make sure my plans and ideas lined up with God's plans for me, and I didn't want to go into something if it wasn't my true calling. So many times, people start businesses, and in a couple of years, they're closing or become burnt out. I just wanted to make sure I didn't fall into either of those categories.

Some people are very lucky to know what they want to

be at a young age. Some might not know until later on in life, and that is okay too. It doesn't matter when your vision comes. The most important thing is that you follow through regardless of what curves life might throw at you. When my vision came for me to become an entrepreneur, my mom was stationed overseas. I sent her a message explaining how I was opening a grooming salon and how I got the vision from JJ. She was super excited. My mom knows I have a habit of starting things and never completing them; I guess it's the Libra side of me. She told me I had a great plan but wanted me to see it through.

Of course, this made me nervous because I didn't know anything about being an entrepreneur, nothing about the pet industry, and I didn't want to disappoint my mom. I knew I had a disadvantage because I didn't attend grooming school or intern with anyone. I looked up multiple private schools to attend, but I couldn't just drop my priorities at home to go away for twelve weeks for school. I had to take this seriously and not fumble the opportunity most are scared to jump into.

In this early phase, be very careful telling your dreams and visions to family and friends. A lot of people will not be happy for you, or they might deter you from your goals. Stay focused and try to keep your goals and vision to yourself until you've completed them all. Yes, you might feel lonely and nervous in this phase, but I promise it will pay off in the end! So, after vision comes the research.

Notes:

1. Where do you see your business one year from now?

2. Where do you see your business five years from now?

3. Do you believe your vision is your true calling? Why or why not?

4. If you have shared your vision with others, what was their response? How did their response impact you?

5. How will you stay focused on your vision to ensure it comes to pass?

RESEARCH

This phase can be overwhelming, but this is the most important phase. Research will be different for everyone, but it's a phase you can't shortcut. Once I had my vision completed, I knew more work was still ahead of me. Research is taking vision to the next level. After dreaming up a great vision of what you want your business to be, the research phase is often the first road-block for many people. It's not enough to just have an awesome idea; you have to lay the foundation. When you start researching, you're taking the first step of confidence towards making your vision a reality. I first started with the location. I knew the area I wanted to be in, so I started shopping—building shopping, that is. I saw this nice four-teen hundred square feet space in a busy Kroger shopping center. It was the first place I checked out. I immediately fell in love with it, and the incentive to move in was pretty sweet too. In 2010, the property manager offered one year of free rent, only paying the common area maintenance charges (CAMs), and ten thousand dollars reimbursement for set-up costs. This was just what I needed, right? Once I asked about the monthly payment, I was a little scared. Sixteen hundred and fifty dollars per month is a lot. I would have to groom a lot of dogs to make this rent, not including utilities, payroll, and personal bills. I decided to take the leap and trust that God wouldn't let me fail. I mean, I had a very aggressive plan to advertise and market to make my business successful. Once you sign your name on that lease, it's set in stone, so if you doubt anything, this is the time to ask and negotiate with the landlord. My landlord was offering a four-year lease but do what's best for you. Consider if you want a short or long-term lease. Just be mindful when you are reviewing your lease, you read it line by line. Make sure to ask any questions you need clarification on.

Who is responsible for property taxes? Who takes care of repairs? Trash service? Can you solicit customers in the parking lot? Will rent remain the same for the duration of the lease? What are the fees for late rent payments? Dogs will be barking, is there a noise ordinance? Can you offer boarding and daycare services? Is plumbing already installed? Are the exit signs visible? How many fire extinguishers do you need for your square footage? How long has it been since the air conditioner and furnace have been serviced? Who is responsible for those repairs? Make sure you have a copy of the lease when you sign. We don't need any problems!

After I found my location, it was time to get nosey. I had to research and see who my competitors were in the area. What are their reviews? What are their prices? What products do they use? It's not enough to focus only on the details of your specific business. You have to take into account the industry, your specific area, and the demographics to see how you can stand out. Everyone doesn't look at grooming the same, and what you bring to the table is what will make you successful, so don't hold back on studying others who are already doing it. I took it as far as calling each shop and asking for different breed prices to make sure my prices were reasonable. I also did a pop-up and checked their shops out while asking for prices. I looked out as far as five to ten miles. At the time, it was a PetSmart and three grooming shops in the area. It didn't matter to me. Once I had my vision in my head, I had to push through. I loved the area, and even though there were other shops, I felt mine was different. It was rough in the beginning because I remember a time when one of the shop owners put false stories out about me and my business. She thought it would hurt me, but in reality, it helped. People started coming and looking to see who I was telling me her stories and fabrications, and now they are my best clients.

Always remember, if you're doing something right, it will upset the HATERS! Just keep in mind people will quickly pick up on your personality when they first meet you and base their conclusion on that first encounter. Always remember that!

Now, I needed to research my business entity (LLC, corporation, sole proprietor), tax identification number, business insurance, and business bank account. It's pretty easy to complete this process. Once that was completed, I needed to head to the city to get my business license. Wow! It's coming together now. We have really done so much up to this point, but it's more.

Like I mentioned earlier, location is important, but not just for traffic and demographic purposes. The place you've found may be in the perfect location and financially on-point for you, but is it zoned by your city for your business?

Don't be caught unaware, especially after you've signed a lease! You can easily avoid this by looking up your city's local ordinances and touching base with your city's zoning or planning department.

You'll also want to start thinking about how to manage the finances of your business. First, I recommend you set up a separate business bank account as soon as possible. Some start out processing business transactions through their personal account, and while you can get by on this for a short period of time, it's best to separate your business from your personal as soon as possible. This will help make tracking your day-to-day sales and expenses a lot easier, and when it's time to do your taxes, it'll make the whole process so much easier.

Visit www.irs.gov for tax id number information and www.sos.ga.gov to register your business with the state of Georgia. If you are outside the state of Georgia, please go to your state's Secretary of State website and look for the business division—as the varies for each state. Visit your local bank to start your business account. Make sure to bring all your documentation.

Checklist:

( ) Register business with the state
( ) Receive EIN
( ) Open a business bank account
( ) Obtain business insurance
( ) Check zoning requirements
( ) Apply for all permits
( ) Put a system in place to check day-to-day sales
( ) Become aware of ALL restrictions and requirements of physical location
( ) Locate and research competitors

Notes:

1. What research have you done thus far?

2. What research do you need to do?

3. Describe your ideal client? Demographic? Spending habits? Likes? Dislikes? Income? Etc.?

4. How will you structure your business? Corporation? LLC? Sole Proprietor? And why?

_____

_____

_____

_____

_____

_____

_____

_____

_____

_____

_____

_____

_____

_____

_____

_____

_____

_____

5. Who are your competitors, and how do you stand out from them?

3

FUNDS

In the research phase, you need to know of how much money you will need to make this vision come to life. It depends on you. I'm pretty sure you can start a business with five thousand and work your way up. But, again, it just depends on the vision you have for your business. Growing up, my mom always told me, "Janelle, you have champagne taste with no money to your name." I knew coming into this I had ten thousand from my 401k, but that wasn't enough. I needed more. The first person I went to was my mom. I asked if she could invest in me or match what I already had. She did that and more. I went to my Uncle John and asked him the same question, and he blessed me with seven thousand dollars. And remember, the landlord was giving me ten thousand dollars back for reimbursement. So, I felt pretty confident going into this thing called entrepreneurship.

If you don't have a family member who can invest in you, the next step will be to look into a bank loan. If you have good credit and a low debt ratio, you can apply for a loan. Keep in mind most banks won't approve loans for start-up businesses, but depending on what amount you need, maybe getting a credit card or a line of credit will help. Securing a business credit card, in particular, is a helpful way to keep your personal and business expenses separate and establish your business credit file. This is what lenders will look at when you get ready to ask for larger loans in the name of your business. Many vendors also offer short-term financing with few requirements in the form of "net 30 accounts." These accounts allow you to purchase products from them and defer payments to a later date. This is one of the most valuable ways to manage your limited business finances, especially when you're first starting out. Credit Unions are a great place to get funding as well. Check with your state to see if they have government funding for grants, especially for minorities and women in business. You'll be surprised what's available.

While those options do depend on your personal credit rating, one of the most popular ways of raising funds that have leveled the business playing field is crowdfunding. Anyone can do it. As long as you're willing to take the time to honestly share your story and how you plan to make good on your vision, you might be surprised at how successful a crowdfunding campaign can be! The most successful attempts start with sharing on social media, so you really can't be afraid to put yourself out there. The trade-off of a little vulnerability for the capital you need is priceless!

Having a business plan is very important. You will need this plan if you're asking for funding from a financial institute. I personally didn't have one until my second year in business, and my Uncle paid for it to be done. I honestly didn't see the need for it. I knew I wasn't going to the banks for funding, and I already knew my daily and monthly goals. This is just my opinion if you have been in business for more than five years and bringing in a profit of over six figures, then yes, you need a business plan. Don't get me wrong, if you do get a business plan starting out and you don't use it to get funding, at least you can review it from time to time to see the numbers as to where you should be with your business and get motivated by it when the slow season approaches.

Business plans can be used as a roadmap to help keep you on track with your mission and help you stay true to your vision. It's all too easy to start out with one idea and start changing things along the way every time a new thought or fad comes along. A business plan kind of acts like an accountability partner. Again, even if you're not using it to get funding, just having a plan to review will always come in handy!

When I first opened my doors on May 18, 2010, I just knew I would come to work with people waiting in line to bring their dog in for grooming. Oh boy, was I wrong. It didn't work out that way. I didn't have my first customer until the end of the month on Memorial Day weekend! I remember thinking to myself, what have I done? It's over. I failed! I couldn't sleep or eat for two weeks. I was so stressed. So many thoughts ran through my head. I felt defeated. That's a feeling I can't explain. It really tests your patience and determination. There's nothing like jumping out on faith and having nothing but hope to assure you that you won't fall. It's a strange contrast of unwavering belief and persistent uncertainty in what you're doing. If I had listened to those doubts, I would have missed out on so much! As tough as it was, I knew where I could go to find encouragement. In those two weeks of being open, I remember praying, asking God not to let me fail. His answer to me was simple, "If you pay me my ten percent, I'll always take care of you." Wow! Really? That's all? That simple? And that's what I did! So, regardless of your faith or religion, you have to find a higher place/source to pull your strength from because being an entrepreneur is not for the weak, and every day will not be peaches and cream. You will be tested daily as to why you started this journey. I wanted to quit and give up multiple times, only to get back up the next morning to start the grind all over again. That's how I could make it eleven years without getting a bank loan or depending on something or somebody else to make it. Strictly depending on God and paying my ten percent, having faith in my passion, and being devoted to my vision, business was good, business was booming, and I was finally in my happy place.

Depending on how you accept payment from your customers, credit card companies offer to fund your business based on your credit card sales. For example, suppose your company makes at least five thousand per month with credit card sales. In that case, you could get working capital from your credit card company for a percentage they take out automatically from your credit card balance at the end of the business day. I was hesitant in my third year of business when this offer was presented to me because I had not heard of it before. But it was legit, and I was excited! It doesn't matter what type of business you are in. Every entrepreneur needs working capital. You can use it however you like: payroll, taxes, bills, equipment, expansion, vehicle, marketing, inventory, uniforms, you name it. Once you pay it back, it will be easier if you want another installment, and you might qualify for more.

In this phase, I wanted to save as much money as I could when I started to shop for grooming equipment. I purchased most of my tables and chairs from Amazon. I purchased the tub at Home Depot and added tile around it to make it decorative. I spent less than three thousand on everything. After a year, I upgraded everything to what I really wanted. If you're looking to start in a shop, I would say don't try and cut corners with your build-out. You want to make sure it's done right, and everything is up to your city's codes. Maybe you are lucky to have a partner or family member who is handy and could help you save money. That would be awesome.

If I could give you one important piece of advice, always keep at least five to ten thousand dollars in a reserved savings account. This is your emergency account. If you don't have it, start saving with a little amount and work yourself up to this. For example, take ten dollars and put it away after every service. Or consider cutting out a small habit, like a daily coffee run, and start saving! You may even have to work a part-time job or groom on your days off. Don't be concerned with how much you're able to put back at any one time. Just do it. This is so important because, as an entrepreneur, things pop up on you all the time. Equipment breaks, and you will have unexpected repairs, or business might be slow, and you still have to function as normal. The objective is to be prepared at all times!

In addition to saving cash before you spend it, also think about ways you can save on the expense you'll already be paying. For instance, turn off your computers when you leave the building for the day to cut down on an unnecessary utility expense. Put your appliances and electronics on power strips instead of plugging them directly into the wall, so at the end of the day, you can turn everything off with one switch and save on your power bill even more. When it comes to equipment, unless it's absolutely necessary, consider buying what you need secondhand. There are so many places to find office supplies that have been gently used. It's almost a crime to spend that extra money when it can be better used somewhere else in your business! During those times when business slows down, you'll be happy you found ways to cut costs.

Nobody told me going into entrepreneurship there would be a slow season. *Like huh? What do you mean?* Some groomers don't experience slow time, but plenty of us do. I learned really quickly that January and February were slow. It picked up March through July. It was slow again in August and September because kids go back to school, then October through December is crazy busy because of the holiday season. And God be with you in November and December because that is the craziest time of the year, but every groomer loves this time because we make so much money. Business usually doubles those two months. That would be a great time to stack your money in the busy months to get you through the slow times.

Notes:

1. What is your plan to fund your business?

_____

_____

_____

_____

_____

_____

_____

_____

_____

_____

_____

_____

_____

_____

_____

_____

_____

2. Do you have a business plan? If no, why not? If yes, are you pleased with it?

3. How much money will you need to maintain your business expenses and overhead for one year?

4. How much money do you need to invest before the doors of your business are open? (Consider permits, vendors, contractors, insurance, etc.)

5. What expenses will you cut in order to save money? After you determine those expenses, how much can you save in one month?

6. How much money do you need to set aside to have six to eight months of expenses?

7. In what ways will you cut expenses in your business without compromising the quality of your services?

4

ADVERTISING AND MARKETING

This is where most entrepreneurs drop the ball. When you open a business, you have to let people know you're there. I don't care if you have a large following on social media; you still have to post daily. You have to get the word to people so they can come and support you. I also learned early on you can't depend on family and friends to support you. I have been blessed to build my company up, so I don't have to rely on people I know to bring their dog to me, and I don't take it personally when they go somewhere else to get their dog groomed. It's all good. We are not in business to beg people to support us. Continue your grind and hustle like you have been doing, and I guarantee those people will see success in you.

So, when you think of marketing and advertising, what do you think of? Newspapers, billboards, social media, mailers, referrals, rewards programs, Google ads, websites? Collaboration with other businesses? There isn't a wrong answer with this because as long as you do something daily and monthly, you will be winning. For me, I wanted to start in my community. I wanted everyone to know Chateau 4

Paws was here! I contacted this lady who had a business where she mailed out your postcards to any zip code for a great price. I did that for four months straight. On that postcard, I advertised "free toothbrushing with this card." I sent over five thousand cards out in a four-month time frame.

Once the word got out that I was there, now I had to keep them coming back. We will talk about that in the next chapter. I also created a referral program. Each time you refer someone, you get five dollars off. Everyone loves a discount, and that worked, but you have to make sure you have a system to keep track of everything. Starting out, I saw that Tuesdays were a slow day for me. After talking to my dad, who had over twenty years of management under his belt, about my slow days, he told me I have to create an offer for my clients no other shop was offering. He always told me, "Janelle, people want to feel like they're getting something for free! Even if they aren't. You need to present it to them as a complete package." He and I both created Senior Day on Tuesdays. If you're over fifty-five years old, you get five dollars off your total bill! Once the word got out that seniors could bring their dogs and get a discount, I was booked every Tuesday. Always remember word travels fast about good service, but it travels faster when service is horrible. Regardless of how many people respond to your offer, keep in mind, always give one hundred percent of your best because you can't be successful if they don't return. We are not trying to be a one-time wonder!

Remember, this is a marathon, not a race! Google became my best friend. I saw that on Google, a lot of people would go and post reviews on their experience at my shop. So, I needed to create content on Google so when someone Googled "pet grooming near me," I would pop up as number one. In the previous chapter, I said I had three other shops I was competing with. Well, my business wasn't in the top three listings. Starting out, my business was at the bottom. It took months, maybe even a year, for me to crawl to number one. We added pictures weekly of our fur babies, clients and asked people to leave honest reviews.

I think Google is the best platform for any business because everyone always has their phones in their hands, and Google gives every piece of information to the public. If you see that your reviews aren't the best, then that's when you need to make some changes in-house. Really consider what the client is saying, and definitely make changes. No matter what your budget is, you have to advertise your business in some way. Get creative. Be bold. Be you.

If I could say what my one downfall is in advertising, it would be social media. I honestly don't have the time to post. I look at other businesses that literally post sales, specials, and promotions all day. And that's awesome, but for me, I just can't get into it. I struggle with content and hashtags. I can't come up with content on a daily. I know my strengths and weaknesses, and you should know yours as well, so this is where I needed to hire someone who was a social media creator and allow them to make my daily post.

Once my clients trust and know me, then they follow me on Facebook or Instagram. I have multiple clients following my personal pages as well. This is tricky because your personal life is just that. But you still have to be mindful of what you post. Customers want to see if you're relatable and get to know you outside your business. It's a catch-22, but you need to live your life. You don't have to post everything. You get it? If you're a business owner, you have to conduct yourself accordingly, even when you're not working. Customers will always have their eyes on you. Just be mindful. But you definitely want to create a business account with Facebook, YouTube, LinkedIn, and

Instagram. I might get a new client on social media, but my focus is on the everyday people who may not have social media.

Billboards are a great way to get people to see you. I tried that on and off for four months. I don't think it really worked for me. I did get a few people, but I would rather spend money on things that people can actually see and hold in their presence. One of my clients asked me if I wanted to advertise on the Kroger Pharmacy bags, and of course, I jumped on that. It was a great turn out too! They printed twenty thousand bags, and once they were gone, that was the end of the offer. I received many calls and new customers from it.

But marketing doesn't stop there. Once the customers were coming in, I made sure their experience was personal, honest, and warm every time. That in itself is marketing at its core: how does your business make them feel when they're there and after they leave? What people say about how you treated them and how you made them feel long after they leave is the most priceless piece of advertising you can ever get.

As you grow, think about how your advertising approach can grow. If you've been relying mainly on word-of-mouth, why not take another step and create a website? If you already have a website, maybe consider setting up social media and having a team maintain it? If your social media is already going strong, how about starting a YouTube channel to show some of the day-to-day fun that happens behind the scenes?

And don't just think about getting the word out to your potential customers. Think about the similar businesses near you, like pet shops and veterinarians. Once you start building relationships, you'll have direct access to exactly the type of customer you're looking for. You could even decide to put on a free joint event with one of these businesses. That's not only a great way to give back to your community; it's free positive brand marketing as well!

All in all, you have to think outside the box and never stop advertising! There are so many other things you can do. Just wearing your business shirt out in public will get people to talk, or having your car wrapped with your company information will get people to call, and the list goes on and on. Keep grinding and never stop because you are in control of your business at the end of the day. What you put in is what you get out of it. Also, be mindful not to compare yourself to anyone else because you'll always question yourself and start to feel like you're lacking, and self-doubt will set in. Social media will have you feeling like you're a failure because of likes and pictures people post glamorizing their life. We need positive vibes only. Everyone will have a different story. Some will get there sooner than others, but we all will cross the finish line eventually.

Notes:

1. What is the marketing plan for your business?

_____

_____

_____

_____

_____

_____

_____

_____

_____

_____

_____

_____

_____

_____

_____

_____

_____

2. How much does it cost to market your business on a monthly basis?

3. How will you enhance your customer's experience so they will be your best word of mouth advertisement?

5

YOUR TOP FIVE

I wish someone would've told me about having a top-five on my team. What's the top five, you ask? The top five is a list of people you need to have in your contact list under favorites.

Lawyer

You need to be in close contact with a business attorney. I mean, so close their number is on speed dial. Why? When you first open your business, some people will look at your place of business as a payday. You might have a situation where a dog gets injured in your care, and the owner wants to take you to court. You need a lawyer who can help you. You also need an attorney to create a waiver for new clients to sign and a non-compete agreement for your groomers if you have any. Any legal question you may have is for your attorney to answer. You might have to pay a retainer for your attorney, but it's something you definitely can't afford not to do.

I had a situation where this client brought her Shih Tzu

in to get groomed. At the time, we didn't know she was cage aggressive. The bather put her in the cage, but we couldn't get her out. This was on a busy Saturday, so we waited and waited for the dog to calm down. After one and a half hours, she was still barking and acting nervous because there were so many dogs that day. The customer decided to pop in and check to see how the dog was doing. I told her everything and let her know she should take her because she was super stressed being there with the other dogs. Once she and I got to the cage because the dog wouldn't let us touch her, the mom immediately saw the dog's eye had popped out of the socket. I was just as shocked as she was. I immediately apologized to her and quickly explained to the customer we never touched the dog, and it was no way this accident was our fault. We reviewed the tapes, and we showed her how we were having a difficult time getting her out. To say the least, she was pissed, and she took the dog to the vet. She came back to the shop with six of her family members, demanding I pay the bill. The bill was four hundred dollars. Of course, I would have paid the bill, but she handled the whole situation wrong. After all of this, I still offered her half of the vet bill to pay. She didn't want that; she wanted it all paid. I felt threatened, and my staff was on edge seeing her whole family barge into the shop demanding money. To make a long story short, she took me to court, and of course, I had my attorney with me. We explained our side, and she explained hers. In the end, the judge ruled I didn't have to pay anything because, on the vet papers, it stated Shih Tzus are common for shallow eye sockets because of their smushed face or bulging eyes. Could I have won this case without an attorney? Maybe so, but I wouldn't have taken the chance. Always lawyer up!

Accountant

This is very important because you need an accountant just as much as you need air to breathe. Your accountant will make sure you don't spend the rest of your life in jail for taxes. Your accountant can do your day-to-day bookkeeping, payroll, make sure your company is efficiently operating, tax returns, finance reports, and accounting records. They do this by accessing your banking financial reports and statements. Your accountant will know federal, state, and local financial, legal requirements by studying existing and new legislation and enforcing adherence to requirements. Mark my words, you don't want the headache of dealing with running a business and worried about the government paperwork. This is why you need an accountant on your team.

Graphic Designer

I was blessed that my best friend's passion is graphic design. I don't think my path would've been easy if she wasn't right there assisting me. If you remember earlier, I spoke briefly about my best friend, Janae, who quit her job around the same time I was fired. Well, Janae was my right-hand girl, my cheerleader, and my business advisor. She basically helped build my company from the ground up. She was there from the beginning to the present day. When starting a business, it can and will be very stressful and challenging. Some days are good, and some aren't, but it's imperative you have someone with who you can bounce your crazy ideas and someone who can lift you when you feel like the world is closing on you.

Why is it so important to have a graphic designer? Because you need this artist to see your vision in the beginning stage of you planning your business. You're trusting them to bring your vision to life. Your artist will create your website, business cards, print designs, t-shirt design, social media content, banners, billboard ads, and much more. Your graphic designer is basically holding your business in their hands and shaping how people view your business.

A strong online presence is essential to the growth of your business. While it's important to make sure you are marketing your company effectively, you must also focus on what your website's visitors see when they come to your home page.

When I wanted to create a marketing campaign, I learned to be mindful not to overwhelm the client. But it's your graphic artist's job to create this for you. Or you might be lucky and are artistic yourself and able to do everything. Good for you! Either way, it must get done in order for your business to survive. I didn't want to have to deal with anything other than the day-to-day business. I couldn't add anything else to my plate, so I gave Janae full control over advertising, marketing, and printing. I gave her my vision, and she took off with it, and I'm happy with the results. Again, do what's best for you and your budget. I took Janae out for lunch and drinks for her payment because she would never charge me. She always said, "If you make it, I make it," and that's how we rolled. Even today, she still doesn't charge me what she should, but I guess that's the perk of having your best friend as your graphic designer! Everyone always tells me I have the best of both worlds. I am lucky to have my best friend ride this wave with me and keep me grounded while still being my hype man and pushing me to new levels. She's the real MVP.

Mentor/Coach

If I had one wish, I would have wished to have a coach in the pet industry I could have talked to. This is a top priority, finding someone you can get advice from who will not sugarcoat the truth to you. A mentor is someone who's been where you've been, knows what strategies to keep you there and what it takes to win. You don't have to speak to your mentor daily but definitely keep them close by and abreast of your business changes and growth. My mentor and coach was my Uncle John. He owns a successful landscaping company in Texas. I can trust he has my best interest at heart, not because we are family but because he truly wants to see me win. He always tells me the truth. Sometimes I don't want to hear it, but I appreciate it because my decision could've been a costly mistake if I hadn't called him. A mentor is there to make your path easier. They can help you avoid certain situations because they have the blueprint of success. It's easy to fall off track, but it's even harder to stay on when you have nobody to push you.

Insurance Agent

In the first year of business, I was a nervous wreck. I wanted to make sure I was protected, double time. Anything that occurred, I would call my agent to let her know of the situation. She had to assure me everything was okay and not to worry so much. I'm thankful I've never had to use my insurance, but I'm grateful that it's there. Make sure to get multiple rates when shopping for insurance companies in your area. You don't want to get caught not having it. This expense is something you need to include in your monthly budget, and you can also write it off at the end of the year. For example, business insurance can help pay the costs of property damage, lawsuits, lost business income, and other covered losses.

Those were my top five, but don't feel like you only have to stick to these types of people. Your five might include a YouTube content creator or a dedicated blog writer. The point is to make sure you surround yourself with a team that will push and support you.

Notes:

1. Who are your top five? If you do not have a top-five yet, who do you want on your team?

2. If you do not have your top five yet, who can you ask for referrals?

3. How much money (on average) per month will you spend on your top five?

4. What type of insurance do you need for your business?

5. What assistance do you require from a mentor?

6

CUSTOMER RETENTION

Customer Retention increases your customers' lifetime value and boosts your revenue. It also helps you build amazing relationships with your customers. They trust you with their money because you give them value in exchange. When I was working at the bank, my manager instilled this phase in my head, "The customer is always right." She told me always to remember that because we work for the people and the people are the ones who keep us working daily. So, I applied that same training to my business. Every client will not be the same. You will have some clients who don't care how you groom their dog. You will have clients who will be very detailed and very difficult, but regardless of who and how they act, our job is still to provide great customer service. Your attitude has to be flexible to assist all types of people. When clients step through your door, nothing else matters. The client should have your undivided attention. Always say thank you, or I appreciate your service. Clients love to know they are appreciated. Once the client has gained your trust and faith, then that's how your business grows—organically and honestly.

I saw that having open communication with each customer is what they valued the most. I take pride in living up to the time I tell the client to return for their dog. But, everyone knows the day can change quickly, and it's our job to communicate with the customer about time changes. A simple phone call explaining you are super busy and running behind goes a long way versus having the client come when you told them and explaining when they are there to come back because their dog isn't ready. What an inconvenience. Or if you accidentally nick or cut a dog, let the owner know so they can monitor it and not hide it from them because they will see it later. Now they are calling you with multiple questions. We are not trying to add any more problems to our plates because we already deal with a lot.

Communicating this information shows your main priority is the health and safety of the pet. I remember when I first started grooming, I had a very active yorkie I had to groom. This day was like the fourth time I had groomed him. Every time I did him, I would get nervous because he was all over the table. This particular time I was finished grooming him but was just looking over his face and trimming what I saw needed to be trimmed. Then out of nowhere, he stuck his tongue out, and just like that, I cut the tip off! I paused in shock and immediately began to cry as the tip of his tongue was on my shears. After I got the bleeding to stop—after roughly thirty minutes—I was thinking, how in the world can I tell the customer this? Then I said to myself, "Janelle, you just gotta tell the truth," and that's what I did. Of course, I was crying when I explained what happened, but the client was not upset at all, and she respected that I told her the truth. So just remember, you will experience different situations, but always keep the door open for communication with the client.

I also try my best to greet each customer when I can. I want to get to know everyone, and I always tell my staff to find something about the client that you can remember about them or their dog to get familiar with them as well. For example, when I'm talking to a customer, I ask multiple questions to remember them. How long have you had your dog? Did you rescue or buy from the breeder? Where are you from? Do you have family here? OMG, you're driving my favorite car; how do you like it? Do you live in the area? These are great questions to get the conversation going. Once you've built a rapport with the customer, they have an idea of who you are as a person, and now they feel comfortable leaving their pet with you.

You might find you have a lot of things in common with your clients. On top of that, it will open so many doors for you. Once you know your clients, you'll see that they are attorneys, doctors, business owners, mechanics, nail techs, and more. My motto is, "If they support me, I'll support them! PERIOD. Whether you're shy or not, you have to know who your supporters are if you want a successful business. The customer just wants to feel spoiled, just like their fur babies, and they want to make sure you have their fur baby's best interest at heart. We also mail holiday cards, birthday cards, give report cards, call the clients when their pet has passed to give them our condolence, and offer a reward program.

Please note that it can be difficult while you're in this phase because you want to please every client. Don't make a mistake like me and give your personal cell number out to clients. You have to create a boundary with your clients. If not, they will run all over you. They will call you late nights and early mornings, weekends, and holidays, just to ask if their dog can be scheduled in. Learn time management and setting business hours with them ASAP and stick with it. Don't answer the phone after hours, and it's okay to reply to their e-mail the following day. We need to normalize creating boundaries and a system!

All in all, remember to focus on what works best for you and your customers by trying out different approaches. Maybe that's writing handwritten notes of thanks and sending them out after every appointment. Or maybe a note to thank your customers for their support during the slow seasons. It could even be surprising them with an on-the-spot discount when they come in for no other reason than because you want to thank your customers on that day. These types of actions will keep your customer base on their toes in a good way and on the lookout for your unexpected appreciation. Not only will they keep coming back, but word will definitely spread about how your business is always thinking about ways to reward them.

I briefly mentioned earlier in the advertising section about creating a YouTube channel. This is an awesome way to keep customers engaged, especially during the slower seasons when life just may not let them get their fur baby to you right away. Don't be afraid of sharing tips about how to keep their fur babies clean when they're not able to get to the groomer. Focus on the differences in types of breeds, talk about why some things work for some and not others, and suggest products you will vouch for. Spotlight different issues that are specific to different animals. Show you and your team preparing for the day and keeping your facilities clean. The goal isn't just to have a lot of videos but to show your customers that you really care about them and their pets, beyond the exchange of money for a service. So many people want to learn more but don't know where to start. What better way to show customer appreciation and guarantee customer retention by providing a solution to another one of their problems?

Notes:

1. What system will you implement to ensure you provide excellent customer service?

2. How will you handle customer complaints?

3. In which ways will you communicate with your customers? E-mails, YouTube, postcards, etc.?

4. How will you train your team to handle your customers? Orientation, hands-on training, workbooks, etc.

5. Will you implement a customer reward or retention program? Explain how the program will work?

7

BUILD YOUR TEAM

Everyone's story will be different, but for me, I had no clue about the pet industry, nor did I have any knowledge about running a business. What I did know is if I hire the correct staff, I should be okay. Right? Well, that wasn't the case. In 2010, I started out hiring a groomer and a bather when I opened. I had no clue what to look for in their work, and my only focus was to schedule the appointments and allow my staff to work. But I learned very soon there were times when the groomer would be late or call out of work. Now, what was I supposed to do? I didn't know how to groom, so I had to explain to the client that I didn't have a groomer, and they had to reschedule. I was not a happy camper. We start a business to make money, not to lose it. After the second time of her calling out, I fired her. I quickly hired another groomer and had the same issue. I fired that one then repeated the hiring process and quickly fired her too. Is this a pattern?

I didn't understand what I was doing wrong and why I had such a hard time finding a good groomer. So, I took things into my own hands. That weekend I went to PetSmart and purchased my own clippers and blades. I devoted that whole weekend to watching YouTube videos on how to groom different breeds. Yes, I went to YouTube University! I'm not ashamed. When Tuesday came, I was a nervous wreck, but I was honest with the client and told them I was a new groomer, and it would take a few hours for their fur baby to be ready, and I'd call them as soon as they were. I took my time and made sure I did my best with grooming. I remember I would get frustrated with completing a teddy bear face. I would often head over to YouTube to look at how to groom a teddy bear face so I could complete the groom. After I saw the customers weren't complaining about my grooms, I started to get more confident. I saw being the primary groomer and having a full-time bather, business was actually picking up. My days were booked, and my Saturdays were completely full. I was so busy I had my boyfriend at the time helping me bathe dogs, and my sister would come and answer the phone and check customers in and out. In that short period of time, I learned you don't have to be the smartest or the best groomer; you just need patience, consistency, hard work, integrity, and dedication. Your customers will see that.

After my family ran away from my calls to come in and work, I knew I had to seek help. I was always told I'm a hard and demanding boss, but I honestly feel you have to be in order to run a successful business. I wasn't in a rush to hire this time, and I knew what questions to ask: *How long have you been grooming? Why did you leave your last job? What breeds can you groom the best? What breeds do you least like to groom? Do you have reliable transportation? Can you groom at least six dogs per day?* Also, in part of the interview, you have to groom three dogs for review. I was ready. I had been grooming by myself for almost two years, and I was ready to expand the team. I understood my talents and strengths, and this groomer had to understand the vision and know I wasn't playing around.

Being an entrepreneur was tough, and I almost burnt myself out because I didn't want to let someone come in and groom. I thought I could handle it all, but it was too much. There weren't enough hours in the day for me to complete my work. I knew I had to hire someone. The signs were bright!

When looking for people to add to your team, make sure you give them an honest layout of your day-to-day duties. Try to be open with them so they know if they can accept or deny the position. *Can they work in a fast-paced environment? Can they work under a strict time frame? Are they comfortable speaking with clients? How do they handle customer complaints? Can they work well wither others? How do they handle aggressive dogs?* Their passion for dogs has to be so strong you can see it a mile away. If you can see it, then the customer can definitely see it. Once you have one, two, five, ten, or more employees, you need to have daily, weekly, or monthly team meetings. You want to make sure you keep the team abreast on breeds, time management, new products, concerns, goals, and safety cautions.

I could have just hired a receptionist to answer the phone and check clients in and out. That would have helped me tremendously, but I didn't stop there. I wanted to be more hands-on and take a proactive approach to market the company, so I spent a lot of time within the community, and I only groom when needed. Once my customers didn't see my face, I noticed they would freak out and not leave their dog. It was a hard transition for the customers to make. Still to this day, I have many clients who only want me to groom their dogs. I saw that it didn't affect the groomer when they asked for me. But, I also made sure I reassured my groomer I appreciate her, and she's a great asset to the company because she is just that awesome! Take a good look at your company and see how adding another person can help you, and I promise it will make your life much better.

It can be overwhelming when you think about bringing somebody else on to what you've worked so hard to build, but if you take the right approach, you, your business, and your customers will all benefit from it. During the interview, try using different methods to get a better idea of the person you're talking to. Instead of just sitting in a room and asking them scripted questions, let them take a personality test. After the initial introductions, set up a tour of the facilities. That way, not only will your potential new hire get a more realistic idea of the work environment, but you'll be able to gauge their comfort level past what they say.

After you interview them, think about if their aspirations line up with what your business needs are. You could find a very experienced groomer, but if they're only looking for a part-time commitment and you know you need someone full-time, don't ignore that important missing piece. On the flip side, if there's someone who is focused on moving up through the ranks, but you need someone just to fill in here and there, take that information into account before you say yes to hiring them. There are plenty of qualified people out there, but if they're not the right fit for you, don't try to force it. Take the time to find the one who will complement your business, not add more stress to it. Ensure you clearly define the responsibilities of the role you are hiring to avoid any potential issues in the future. Let them know exactly what's expected, and be able to answer questions about every part of the job.

As important as the personality side is, don't forget about some of the technical and legal aspects of the hiring process. One of the best ways to ease your mind is to perform a background check. You also need to check if they are eligible to work in the United States by having them fill out an I-9 and providing valid ID documents as well as employment authorization. You'll want to check your state's requirements to find out if your business needs to enroll in the E-Verify program as well. Not checking this eligibility can put your business in danger of fines or even criminal penalties.

Notes:

1. What positions do you need on your team?

2. How do you plan on sourcing your team?

3. Explain your hiring protocol.

_____

_____

_____

_____

_____

_____

_____

_____

_____

_____

_____

_____

_____

_____

_____

_____

_____

_____

_____

4. For each position that you're hiring for, do you have a training manual or a standard operating procedure (SOP) manual to provide them?

5. Write down at least five appropriate questions you will ask during your hiring process.

8

MULTIPLE STREAMS OF INCOME

L et's be honest, in today's time, everyone has a side hustle, aka another stream of income. Nine out of ten people are working a nine to five, and once they get off, they're working their side hustle. Having another stream of income isn't bad. It's very smart because you want to have at least seven streams of income coming in monthly, so you're not stressing about your main job. For example, full-time students might have a side hustle with braiding girls' hair for a discount, a teacher's side hustle could be tutoring on the weekends, and the local Home Depot guy might have a side hustle cutting grass on his off days. If you aren't working a side hustle, you could be investing your funds in a portfolio, CD, or IRA. You could have a rental property that's making you money per month, and the list goes on and on. For me, it took me five years to decide my hustle. I didn't want to do anything I wasn't passionate about because I feel like you have to have passion for what you want to do in order for you to be successful. I needed to be driven and motivated. Before I do anything, I pray and ask God to reveal what he wants me to do and how I need to do it. I always seek God first. I then noticed customers would ask me, do I offer boarding services? Okay, this might be good. I started to research to see if this was a service I should offer, and I was five years too late.

People are always leaving to go out of town for either personal or business reasons. Why didn't I think of this before? That was my first stream of income. Just on boarding, without advertising, the first year, I made an extra six thousand dollars. Once the word got out the following year, I had almost doubled that. I call that my easy play money because boarding is the easiest service you can offer. Of course, you want to make sure your insurance policy is up-to-date, have working cameras so you can monitor your facility when you're away, and you want to have it comfortable for the fur babies when they are there.

My second stream of income was candles. I always loved candles. Growing up, my mom would always tell me not to leave the candle burning because I might burn the house down—I was known to fall asleep with the candle burning. So, I wanted to create a candle line for my clients. I ran the thought with Janae, and she immediately fell in love with the idea. We basically created this candle with my clients and my love for candles in mind. It's a Pet Odor-Eliminating Candle called PawAroma. I have different scents available online on my website, and I also list them on eBay. My customers love the candles, and I use them in my house for personal use. I'm just feeding into my hobby, which actually pays me.

My third stream of income is teaching students how to groom. Over the years, I would teach my bathers, who would show interest in grooming. This is a tricky hustle because once I taught them the business and how to groom, they would stay with me for a couple of months or years and leave. After the second time that happening, I started to charge. My staff would always ask me if they could learn, and I would say of course and charge a small fee. I saw that once they had to pay, they took the course seriously. I can honestly and proudly say that two people I taught how to groom and color now have successful grooming businesses in the Atlanta area. I pat myself on the back for that! Is this a service that I advertise? No, because I only do it for people I know, and they have to get their hands-on training at my salon.

Another easy stream of income could be driving for Uber or Lyft on the weekends. In 2019, I was going through a divorce, and my money was really tight from paying my attorney. One of my customers suggested I drive for Uber to make extra money, I did. It was cool to get some extra funds on the side, and I also used it to pass out my business cards to riders.

In March 2020, the whole world shut down due to Covid-19. Many people lost their jobs, and a lot of small business owners had to close their doors for good. I, too, had to close my shop for a while and had no money coming in. I had to pull from my savings account to pay bills and rent at the shop regardless of if I was there or not. Luckily for me, I still had my business when so many other businesses had to close. It was a horrible time for everyone; it was the worry of the unknown. *How are we to live and take care of our families when the world is shut down?* People had so many questions and concerns.

Millions of people had to apply for unemployment assistance. I tried my best not to apply, but I needed the help and like many others, I started to panic. What if I had not driven for Uber? If I didn't have that stream of income, I don't think I would have qualified for the help as fast as I did. I'm grateful I was approved with no issues. That's the importance of having another stream of income. In case something happens, you'll be okay financially.

Because of the shutdown, if you had a business, the Small Business Administration (SBA) allowed people to apply for a business grant and loan. This allowed business owners to get funding for payroll or business expenses. SBA was offering one thousand dollars per employee, and that was in the form of a grant, no repayment, and they also were approving people for business loans with low-interest rates and no payment for twelve months. Now that was amazing. Can you imagine receiving funds like this in the middle of a pandemic? How could this help you, your business, your staff, and your family? So many loan options were available to small business owners to take advantage of. It was really a win-win for everyone. I hope you were able to benefit as well.

But maybe you're reading this, and you've just started, or you're about to start, so you can't quite qualify for the SBA grant. Don't worry. There are still other resources you can consider. For grants, check out www.grant.gov. This federal government site offers one of the most complete lists of grants available, and it's constantly being updated. Don't stop there, though. Make sure you search through your state and local governments as they offer specific grants as well. In addition, some major companies and nonprofits offer grants for small businesses to anyone who will apply. A lot of times, all you have to do is enter the information about your business, and they review who they want to give grants to. You never know what opportunity could be the one to help launch your business to the next level!

Notes:

1. Name at least three additional streams of income you can
start.

2. Do your research and write down at least three grants you can apply for.

3. How would a grant of $20,000 help your business?

_____

_____

_____

_____

_____

_____

_____

_____

_____

_____

_____

_____

_____

_____

_____

_____

_____

_____

_____

4. In your own words, why is having multiple streams of income important?

5. What is your backup plan if your business shuts down due to something out of your control?

_____

_____

_____

_____

_____

_____

_____

_____

_____

_____

_____

_____

_____

_____

_____

_____

_____

_____

9

STAY MOTIVATED

L et's face it. Everyone is not blessed to be their own boss. Everyone is also not able to continue to stay in business. This business is cutthroat, and it's not for the weak. You have to be one thousand percent committed to your brand and yourself every day. There are no days off, but you do have to take some time out for yourself at some point. Find something that you love to do like yoga, working out, baking, cycling, etc. Once you take the time out for yourself, you return to work refreshed and ready to work. Be mindful that life changes happen (family issues, death, financial problems, etc.). Don't allow it to deter you or slow you down from completing your dream. You must always remember your Why and your Vision.

Your 'why' is what drives you to keep going in spite of the many obstacles you go through. Each person's Why will be different. Your Why may be to create a legacy for your kids. Someone else's Why could be they love being their own boss. There are millions of reasons why someone does something, and that's okay. Your why should be personal and something that motivates you.

Your vision is how you see your business in a few years based on your goals and aspirations. Your vision statement should inspire yourself and your staff. Your vision should be written down so others can read it and become motivated. As your business grows, you should periodically look at your vision statement to check in on your progress and success. As you become closer to achieving your vision, you can update it to match where you see your business growing in the future. The vision can be forever growing.

Something that helps me stay motivated is I have positive sticky notes on my bathroom mirror and in my closet at home. I have my goals listed, motivational quotes, and scriptures that help me get through my rough times. I also listen to motivational podcasts. Trust me, finding something that brings you peace in a chaotic world will help you so much.

I've outlined my journey to starting my pet grooming business. I'm a successful small business owner in an area I love. I have many people who have been supporters of my dream and continue to support me. Many of my early clients, as I stated earlier, remain with me today. I am hoping this book will spark your desire to execute your plan and dream of entrepreneurship. Continue to stay focused and always remember YOU GOT THIS!

1. Name at least three things you will do to keep yourself motivated.

2. What is your why?

_____

_____

_____

_____

_____

_____

_____

_____

_____

_____

_____

_____

_____

_____

_____

_____

3. What is your vision for your business?

_____

_____

_____

_____

_____

_____

_____

_____

_____

_____

_____

_____

_____

_____

_____

_____

_____

_____

10

GROWTH

Often, when we start a new business, we always see and picture the end results. However, rarely do we picture the work that has to be put forth in the middle to get you to the finish line. However, growth and expansion might not be for every entrepreneur, and that's okay. But, if it's what you want to pursue as the next step in your entrepreneurial journey, then the grind will not stop. Someone once told me, "It might be hard to make your first one hundred thousand, but it's even harder to keep it and double it.

As this year 2021 is closing to an end, I'm in the process of starting my mobile business. When I started this journey, I only wanted a pet spa inspired by my fur baby JJ. That vision evolved into providing boarding services and the development of a candle line. Though I considered establishing a second location for daycare and boarding, going mobile seems like the next move towards growth and expansion. Yes, as a small business owner, it's been a rough road, but I followed the steps outlined in this book and made sure I took my time not to rush the process. It also helped that I have multiple grooming friends with whom I can bounce my questions and ideas.

As I focused on expanding my pet spa services to a mobile option, the most challenging step was finding the right van. I had heard so many horror stories regarding buying used vehicles that it took me five months and over ten car lots to find the right van for me. Then, right when I was thinking about giving up and postponing my mobile business, I saw a guy selling shuttle buses online for dirt cheap. The price was so cheap I honestly thought he was a scam, but I couldn't pass up on the offer. It turned out the bus offered more than what I was initially looking for and was the perfect match for the expansion of Chateau 4 Paws' Mobile Spa. I have no doubt if I use the same formula that brought success to my brick-and-mortar location and avoid the pitfalls, the mobile extension will bring its own level of success.

While there isn't a sure way to ensure your success, you can follow the advice within this book to help you along your journey. I'll recap some of them below.

Focus on your customers and their experience. If you're honest and deliver quality services and products, your clients will quickly spread the news on how good you are. But, make their experience a bad one, and word will spread even quicker. A customer's interaction with your business can make or break your business. You may get clients, but with a bad experience, they may never return.

Hire the right staff and train them to your standards. As an entrepreneur, it's easy to get caught up in the vision. But, if you don't hire the right people to align with your vision and train them properly, then your vision may never come to pass. Your clients not only interact with you, but they interact with your staff as well. You want their interaction to be just as pleasant as if they were interacting with you.

Establish multiple streams of income within your business. 2020 showed us that life can be unpredictable, and your way of life can change without notice. One way to help protect your financial means of living is to have multiple sources of income. This doesn't mean you need to have several businesses. It means you need to have more than one way to make money in your business.

Your top five team. You won't know everything there is to know about business. That's why it's essential to have your top five team. People that will help you in various areas of your business. Whether it's an attorney, accountant, mentor, accountability partner, graphic designer, or business consultant, it's going to help your business out in the long run when you have a great team in place.

Promote yourself and your business. Word of mouth is great, but you also want to ensure that you are consistently promoting yourself and your business. You can do this in multiple ways, such as via social media platforms, Google, SEO, billboards, postcards, print advertisement, or emails.

In a nutshell, starting a business can be scary and filled with uncertainty. Jumping into the unknown is daunting. You will doubt yourself at times, but you have to have the tenacity to keep pushing and not allow those doubts to turn into fear. Or fear to suck the life out of your dream. With vision, research, and a solid implementation plan, I found success as a business owner doing the very thing I was passionate about. You, too, can become the next successful entrepreneur if you believe in yourself and don't give in. So, go out there and start walking into your purpose. Don't let anyone deter you...you got this!

Made in United States
Orlando, FL
18 January 2022

13650383R00057